NANI'S TALE

Corey Fair

Just Write Publishing

This is a work of fiction. Any character references or likenesses to persons living or dead are completely coincidental. Actual people and places have been added to give the story a sense of reality.

JUST WRITE
PUBLISHING
justwritepublishing@yahoo.com

Dedications

I would like to dedicate this to all of the people in this world, men and women alike, who have overcome a tragic situation. Despite the obstacles, they faced their fears, problems, and disadvantages and overcame them, or hopefully one day will.

Contents

Acknowledgements

//

I would like to thank God for giving me the gift of creation to even bring this story to you.

I would like to thank my father for all of his help and support through this whole process and throughout my life.

I would like to thank the women who shared private parts of their lives to help me tell this story.

I would also like to thank the countless family members and friends who have supported my art that I couldn't list here. (Just too many.)

And last, but certainly not least, I would like to thank you for reading my art.

Prologue

Let me start by saying I hate Calvin Smith, AKA Cal. I think he hates me too; he has to. I'm his eleven year old stepdaughter, Nani. He hits me, burns me, and he even molested me before. A lot more than once actually. My no good dope whore momma, Theresa, lets him too!

My dad went off to prison before I was born. He got thirty-five years. I've never met him, saw him, or talked to him before, but I know that however bad he is, he has to be better than Calvin. He just has to be.

No, I'm not a crack baby. My mom started doing heroin when I was two years old. That's also when she met no-good Calvin. He must know magic or he's a wizard or something. He can get my mom to do anything he wants. It's unbelievable! The only reason I do good in school is because I hate being home, if that makes sense to you. I'm only eleven years old, and I hate my life. I can't wait to graduate college and become a famous singer or actress. I don't care which one. I'ma get me a cute, smart, nice husband that can beat Calvin up too!

It's crazy because if you didn't know Cal you'd think he was selling dope instead of using it. He has money, plus he dresses nice, but he doesn't work. He got a huge inheritance when his dad died. He don't do nothing but shoot dope, get drunk, beat me, and boss my mom around. He also eats, poops, and, of course, he sleeps too. Then again, everyone does.

I love it when he's asleep or too drunk to bother me. I'd kill Calvin if I could. I honestly would, but I just don't have it in me. I've seen enough prison shows to know I don't like prison. It's like a hundred Calvins in there and that would just make my life worse. What a thought! I guess we'll never know, at least, I hope we won't.

Well, let me get to the point. I just want to vent and tell my story. That's all. Let me take you back to when my mom first met Calvin, before the beatings and everything else started.

Chapter
01

even though I was only two, I remember the first time I
met Calvin. I thought he was our superhero at first, but
as it turned out, my mom let The Devil into our lives.
He was like a knight to me. He was the perfect gentle-
man. He smelled good, looked nice, and even dressed
nice.

I remember I was fussing over a princess-wrapped
candy bar that I wanted from the front stand in the bus
station. I didn't eat at all that day, and I was cranky,
tired, and hungry. Plus, I loved princesses. At the time,
I didn't understand that my mom needed money to buy
it. Money didn't mean anything to me, and maybe if

we would've had some, my life could've turned out better, or at the very least, different.

Next thing I knew, I started wailing and crying, flapping my arms up and down in a fit. It was my way of releasing "baby" stress, as my mom called it. Being told no can be hard on a kid.

"Nani! Nani! Stop it!" My mom screamed like a tired woman who had just worked a 12 hour shift at Denny's. "God damn it, Nani, why you acting like this? Ughhh! Little girl, I swear!"

"Aghhh! Aghhhh! Aghhhh!" I cried out.

Looking back, I bet that was very embarrassing for her. Even though her hair was long and scruffy-and she looked worn and tired out, she still was a beautiful woman. She was a tall, slender, athletic built, butter pecan colored Puerto Rican and Black woman. My dad is Italian, by the way. Anyway, in the middle of my fit a very tall light skinned man with short hair appeared. He just so happened to be Calvin. He was like an angel at the time.

"Shhh shhh shhhh. Stop all that crying, pretty little girl," he said as he handed my mom the pink princess wrapped candy bar.

My eyes followed it from his hand to hers. My crying ceased immediately. When my mom opened the candy bar and fed me piece by piece, all I did was stare at him in amazement. I thought he was a hero, but really, it's not that hard to trick a helpless woman and a crying two year old. All he was, as it turns out, was a spoiled buster preying on weak women.

"You like that, Sugar Mama? Is that all you wanted, little girl?" Calvin said with an inviting smile on his face.

All I did was stare at him with a messy, wet, happy face.

"What's her name?" Calvin asked my mom about me.

"Nani," she replied.

"That's a beautiful name, and the beautiful woman who birthed her is…?"

"Theresa."

"Theresa," he whispered to himself. Then with a smile on his face, he whispered, "Saint Theresa."

"I'm no saint, but you are. Thank you so much," Mom told him.

"You're very welcome," Calvin replied.

"Bus number seven!" a man yelled out.

"Oh, shit! I gotta go!" Mom shouted.

And with that being said, my mom snatched me up to run off with me in her arms to the bus. I didn't see it, but I can imagine the dumbfounded look on Calvin's face. Later, I learned his expressions very well.

"Wait! Wait!" he yelled behind my mom.

It was pointless though. His screams fell on deaf ears. Theresa A. Vasquez was on a mission. Embarrassing as it is to tell it now, I held out my little hands to him as my mom brought me further and further away from this wonderful candy-giving man. I wanted to cling to him. It was only natural, and I wanted some fatherly love.

As we barely made it on the bus, all I could do was picture that moment over and over in my head. Then, my little belly started to rumble again. I couldn't do anything about it at that moment, nor could anybody else. So I just looked out the window at the trees, businesses, houses, and people we passed on the way to our next destination: Walmart.

I still can't believe I used to think it was a giant house. It didn't look like one, but I couldn't help but think that. When we were getting off the bus there was a gang of people that got off with us. My mom rushed to the nearest basket.

"Come on, Na-Na. We almost there, Mami." she said more to herself than me.

When my mom rolled me into Walmart in that basket, I entered a whole new world. I saw big bright lights and a lot of people with other kids like me, well, at least my same age. I saw a lot of candy, food, clothes, toys... the works. I saw much more, but I was amazed with just the stuff that I already knew of.

I didn't know how long we actually were in the store, traveling around and grabbing stuff before my mom got into the checkout line. While we were waiting, I kept hearing that scanner noise. "Duuuup duuuup duuuuup!" I started looking around when my eyes fell on another princess wrapped candy bar. I got all excited and my eyes got really big. My mom saw my gaze locked onto the candy bar. She rolled her eyes and let out a breath before she handed it to me. I kept fiddling with it and putting it in my mouth trying to open it. Obviously, I didn't succeed. By the time it was our turn, the lady at the register was smiling at me.

"You have a beautiful daughter, ma'am."

"Thank you," she replied.

"Hey, pretty girl," the lady said to me.

"Wave at her, Nani. Say hi," my mom told me.

"Hi," I mumbled.

I was focused on that candy bar. Forget that lady.

"I'll take that for you," the lady said to my mom.

"No, it's ok. I'll handle it. She got all her baby germs on it," Mom said in an apologetic voice.

Next thing I knew, my mom snatched the candy bar from me real fast. She gave the lady a new one from the stand.

"Your total comes to 98 dollars and 58 cents, ma'am."

My mom swiped a blue card across a gray box. I now know that the blue card was a food stamp card. I also know now that it wasn't hers.

"Ma'am, this card only has $52.70 on it," the cashier told my mom.

"No, that can't be. Let me try it again," Mom said in disbelief.

She did try again. The lady pressed a couple of buttons and said "same thing."

"That bitch!" My mom mumbled to herself when she realized that her friend Rhonda had duped her.

Now, here comes a Theresa special.

"No. No. That can't be right. Please call a manager," Mom requested.

"Hold on," said the cashier.

That's when the lady made the mistake of turning around to talk on the store phone. My mom ran off with the cart full of groceries and me in it. Why? I don't know. If she really would've thought that out, then she would've realized that she had nowhere to run. She didn't have a car. We came on the bus. But what do you know? As the lady was screaming and yelling after us, we ran smack dab into Mr. Super Hero, Calvin himself. We ran him over, in fact, but by that time the store security guard had caught up with us. Old Calvin was quick on his feet.

"It's ok. It's ok. She's with me," Calvin told the security guard.

"Oh? So you plan on going for theft too?"

"Theft?" Calvin said with a raised eyebrow. "Naw, there's no theft here. She called me to come bring her the money."

"Wow! What a wise ass chuck," one of the security guards said.

"So, how much does she owe?" asked Calvin.

"Well, I don't know, Captain," one of the officers replied.

"My name is Calvin, Mr. Calvin Smith," he said as he looked at my mom.

"$98.58," she replied in a hoarse whisper.

I know she had to be ashamed. Calvin looked at the officer. "See? I got that." Then he pulled out a $100 bill.

After everything was handled, Calvin walked us to his car.

"Why you always seem to be around? You stalking me?" my mom asked.

Calvin laughed at that, but he didn't know my mom well enough at the time to know that she was serious.

"I don't know, baby girl, but, no, I'm not stalking you. Although, it would probably be enjoyable," he said with a chuckle.

At that, my mom put a questioning look on her face. "That's not funny, uhhhh, Calvin," she told him.

"Look, for some reason I keep coming to the rescue. Maybe the next time I see you it could be on better terms."

"You asking me on a date or something? Because, I don't do dates. I got way too much going on to have a man in my life right now," Mom rambled.

"That's understandable. But seems to me a man is what you need. A man wouldn't have you out here stealing food from a Wal-Mart with yo daughter with you. No offense. I'm just saying," Calvin preached in a hyped tone.

He's good ain't he?

"Why?" asked Mom.

"Why not?" replied Calvin.

"Ughh, Look, you're handsome, and I appreciate you helping me, but I don't know. I got a daughter," Mom told him.

"Ma, I can see that you're beautiful, and you deserve better than how you're living. It couldn't hurt to try me out," Calvin solicited.

Yes, it could and it did.

"I guess," Mom said.

"You guess what?" asked Calvin.

"I'll give you my number. It's getting late and I gotta catch this bus," Mom said in an escaping voice.

"I can drop you off," pushed Calvin.

"That's a definite no. Just call me tomorrow night," replied mom. Calvin pulled out his phone, and my mom punched in her number.

"Bye, Sugar Mama," said Calvin to me with a smile.

And that right there was the first time we met Calvin, and let his evil self into our lives. My mom and Calvin talked on the phone for almost two weeks before they went out on a date. Don't know where they went, nor do I care, but that date sealed the deal. He had her. So, that means he had me too. At that moment he was still the light of our lives. But when he started to come around more, I started to feel weird, and I didn't know why.

Chapter
02

e lived in a small two bedroom house. It was one level, and had no upstairs or basement, but the back-yard was a nice size for me to run around in. Our alley smelled horrible though. Even though our neighbor-hood had stray cats and dogs, gunshots and trash, it was all normal to me. It didn't faze me. We weren't living in the projects, but it sure was the slums. You want to know something, though? I was happy there, at least, at first.

"Hey, Sugar Mama," Calvin said as I rushed into his arms when he came through our door. His face was a regular sight now.

"Hi, Cal," I said with a finger in my mouth.

"Where's ya mom at, Sweetie?" he asked.

"In the potty," I replied in an innocent voice.

"Oh, she in the potty?" he said, mimicking me.

"Mmhm," I responded bobbing my head up and down.

"Let's go surprise her," he suggested.

"'Kay."

When Cal opened the door, you could hear the water behind the curtain bouncing off of my mom and see the steam from the shower.

"Nani?" she yelled.

"Naw, baby, it's me. You supposed to be ready."

"Cal, you got to be at least an hour early. Now, I'm in the shower boy, go on."

"You just need to hurry up," Cal told her.

"I can if you go on somewhere," she said.

"I'll be waiting," he said as he shut the door. While he was waiting on my mom, he sat there on the floor and played toys with me. He even played with the dolls. That night they ended up leaving me alone at the house. They came in real late that night too.

My mom busted through the door, laughing. "Cal, you is crazy!" She paused for dramatic effect. "Baby! Nani, Mami, come here!"

Next thing I knew I was on the floor being smothered in kisses. She had a sweet, stinky smell to her breath. She started rocking me on her shoulder as she walked me to my pink bed. She tucked me in, and then ran a hand across my hair.

"Mami loves you, baby. Never forget that. Night, night."

"Don't let the bed bugs bite!" I continued.

"That's right, baby. Now sleep tight," she told me in a gentle voice.

"Muah!" we both said as we puckered our lips.

I drifted off into a nice, peaceful sleep shortly after that. The next morning, I woke up to see her and Cal laid out sloppily on the floor. When my mom finally woke up, she cooked everyone breakfast. After that, Cal was gone. That same night however, the same situation played back out. He came over, they left, and they came back late. This time, I wasn't in the living room waiting. I was asleep in my bed. My mom had fed me some Nyquil before they left.

Later on that night, I was awakened by moans, slaps, and screams. I first heard it on the other side of my wall. I got up kind of confused, curious, and scared. I slowly walked to my mom's bedroom door to try to open it. It was locked. I heard, "Oh shit, Cal! Oh shit! Yessss. Fuck me!"

SMACK!

"Ah oh ohh my gaaaa! Ohh!"

"Shut up!"

I had thought they were arguing. I went back to my bed that night and stayed up all night long. Even though Cal did nothing wrong, I felt weird and uncomfortable around him from that moment on.

A couple of weeks had passed since that night, and it was finally time for my third birthday party, which wasn't even going to be a real party. I was still excited even though dope whore and Calvin wouldn't allow me a moment of bliss. You won't believe what they did at the party. They did drugs right in front of me on my third birthday! I didn't know exactly what it was they were doing, but somehow I knew it was wrong.

I had also run into more sex episodes. My mom was losing herself. I didn't know what was going on back then. Now that I do, I hate her. Well, I guess I don't really hate her, but I am angry and upset with her. Calvin though? Yeah, him I hate.

At my third birthday party there were two women I didn't know, a man, another little girl like me, Calvin, my mom, and me. I got a bunch of presents. I even had a nice cake. I actually had fun, at least up until that night. I guess the grown-ups thought we were too young to remember or maybe they thought we wouldn't know that they were doing drugs in front of us. They were half right. I didn't know, but I sure do remember.

The whole time me and the other little girl were drinking juice they must've been getting tipsy. They were play smacking, laughing, and just being loud.

"Bring that sugar out, J-rock!" a fat, dark-skinned lady said.

"It's the real party now," someone else said.

"Toot-toot, baby!" the other lady said.

J-Rock pulled out a bag of heroin (I figured out later) from his pocket and then dumped it on the table. He started dividing it up in small lines. Each one of them snorted the powder up their noses. After a while, they were like zombies. My mom was a whole different person. She was nodding, her speech was slurred, and she kept touching herself all over. Once again, I didn't really know what was going on, but I was scared and didn't feel right.

I left the other little girl in the living room to go cry on my bed. I cried that night so much my nose was stuffy and my head hurt. The next morning, Cal woke me up to breakfast in bed.

"Hey, Sugar Mama. Wake up, baby," he said.

I woke up to the old Calvin I knew, not the monster from last night.

"You like yo party yesterday, little girl?" Calvin asked.

"Yeah!" I said in a baby voice.

"Mommy cooked us breakfast. You hungry?" he asked.

"Yeah," I replied.

"Ok. Look what we got here for you. We got eggs, bacon, pancakes with all the gooey, icky sticky stuff you like, and a cupcake full of sugar for my Sugar Mama," he told me in a fatherly voice.

"Thank you, Cal," I said with a big smile on my face.

"Now let's go use the potty and brush them stinky little teeth before you eat. Ok?" he asked.

"Ok!" I responded.

This was the Calvin I liked. This is the Calvin I wish I could remember. We can't always have what we want though, right? The nice Calvin didn't last too much longer, nor did the mom that I used to love. As time moved on, so did I. Their habits of carelessness did also. I had a small concept of what drugs were now, and I also knew that my mom and Cal did them.

They didn't care if I was around or not. Calvin didn't care because I wasn't his child; at least that's what I assumed. My mom didn't care because she was too far gone in the world of drugs. It's a shame I had to see what I did. I wish I could've had someone at that time to take me away, but nobody was around except my mom. I had no dad, no granny, no aunt, no nothing. I had no one that could or would care for or about me.

As my knowledge grew, so did my want for a real dad. I started to wonder why I didn't have one. As time progressed, I would bug my mom about my dad. Either she would give me some BS runaround, or Cal would say *he* was my dad. As if! It's funny. Well, sad really, how when my mom started shooting dope she'd also shoot me what I thought was the truth about my dad.

Calvin and my mom were in the bathroom doing whatever they were doing, and I was in the living room watching a Disney channel show. On the show, *That's So Raven*, Raven had her father. I just sat there and thought, *Why can't I have one and be happy?* I started pouting to myself, and then I became angry. I was so angry that I marched over to the bathroom door as fast as my little feet could carry me.

When I opened the door, the lights were off and they had candles lit. They were butt naked in the tub. I didn't even care because I wanted answers— real ones. During my stare down, my mom was bent over with her butt in the air, fucking Calvin's face. He slapped her butt cheeks then shot a needle in. After he did that, he gave me a hard look and said, "Get yo little ass outta here, Sugar Mama!"

"I want my dad!" I told him.

"I am ya dad. Now go on!" he said.

"No!" I yelled.

"Get yo ass outta here, now!" he said in demanding voice.

"You're not my dad!" I told him.

With that being said, Cal pushed my mom over and then leapt out the tub to grab me. Before I could even begin to run, he reached me and lifted me up in the air. He was screaming at me, and I was terrified. I would've peed my pants if I had had to pee.

"You wanna know where yo daddy at huh? Huh? Yo daddy dead. The sorry bitch is dead!" he said.

"Aaaaayiahhhh!" I screamed in his face with tears in my eyes.

My mom came crawling on the floor behind him wrapping her arms around his ankles.

"Calvin, baby. Calvin! Let her down. Let her down, baby!" she pleaded.

"Get off me, bitch!" he said as he snuffed her on her forehead with the heel of his foot. "I'm yo damn daddy!" Calvin yelled at me before he let me fall to the floor.

He stormed out of the bathroom in a rage. With some of the candles still lit and with water all over the floor, my mom and I laid on the floor, crying in the darkness. She came to cradle me against her naked body, rocking me back and forth while kissing me on the top of my head.

"It's ok, baby. It's ok. Everything's gonna be ok," she whispered to me.

"Your daddy's away in jail, baby. He's in a bad place. He's gone, Mami," she said.

"Where's jail?" I asked her.

"Far away, Mami." she replied.

"I wanna go. I wanna go see my daddy," I demanded.

"One day, Nani, one day," she said in a comforting voice.

That was a lie. But I guess she had to comfort me the best way that she could. I started letting the daddy situation go for a while, but when a program came on the TV one day showing how prison life was, I didn't want to go there, and I didn't want my daddy to be there. Prisons were filled with a bunch of scary looking men, according to TV, of course.

I looked funny at every man that had my skin tone, and I couldn't help but wonder if they were my father. I began watching prison movies and TV shows faithfully after that though. I saw some pretty crazy stuff. It even terrified me a little bit. I just hoped that my dad was one of the tough ones instead of a punk.

Chapter
03

year later, I was turning four years old. Technically, as of midnight on April 14th, I was four years old. Imagine that. It was a year of violence, sadness, drugs, arguments, and worst of all, wanting a father. Believe it or not, I was still excited about my birthday party. Funny thing was, there wasn't one. Little ol' Sugar Mama never saw a party. Dumb, dumb, and dumber set the house on fire somehow. I was asleep when it happened. I was in a deep dream. You know, one of those dreams where you can feel everything, and in my dream, it was dark and moist. It felt like I was in a really hot cave. I started to sweat, panic, and cough. When I started panting, I awoke to smoke. Big black, thick smoke was in my room. Not only that, but there was a real live fire, a super-hot fire. I thought I was still dreaming, and I thought I was in hell. My skin felt like a million fire ants were biting me. My eyes were hurting and stinging. I thought I was going to die, especially when I started choking. I began to fade away into blackness, up to the point of no return.

When I woke up, I was in a room with white walls, a big window with a view of the city, and a greenish blue curtain covering half of the window. My mom and Cal were there along with a few other people I didn't know. I wasn't sure if they were doctors, nurses, or drug friends of my mom and Cal's. I didn't care though. I was high and groggy the whole time I was in the hospital. I was so shell shocked that I was oblivious to the whole world around me.

I started having nightmares about that night, and I still have them sometimes to this day. That was over seven years ago. After we left the hospital, it was confirmed for me that that night had not been a dream. Calvin got us a few pairs of clothes, and some shoes too. He also bought everything else we needed. I found out later that we were homeless because stupid Calvin and Theresa were doing drugs and set the house on fire. Then come to find out, the bastards basically left me to die. They weren't the ones who had saved me. The firemen did.

Even though drugs caused all the hell in our lives, they still chose to dabble with them at the hotel. The hotel room in itself was nice. It had two beds, a flat screen TV, desk, table, plus fancy décor, but it was junky because of us. There were clothes, pizza boxes, and wrappers everywhere. I guess they must've been denying the room service or something.

Calvin was drinking a beer while smoking a cigarette when he looked at my mom who was drugged up in the corner. He had a look of disgust on his face. I'd even go as far as to say it was hatred.

"This all yo fault, you dumb bitch!" he scoffed to himself and continued. "Stankin' ass dope whore Theresa. Bitch, you know my wife left me because of you?" he said in a sickened voice.

My mom finally looked at him in her daze with a slight smile and a look of admonishment on her face.

"Yo wife left you because of you, bitch," she smirked.

Calvin jumped out of his seat with the quickness of a cat and raised his eyebrows.

"You think that shit funny? Huh?" he asked her.

Then my mom started to giggle. She made him feel small and insecure, maybe even insignificant.

"Yeah, I think it's funny. I think you funny," she told him with sarcastic laughter.

"You think I'm funny?" he asked. That took him back a bit. "So, me buying you all these clothes, giving you a place to stay and feeding you is funny to you? Huh?" Calvin inquired.

My mom then nodded her head with a huge smile on her face. Not the type of smile that showed all your teeth, but it still set Calvin off.

"Bitch!" he screamed before he smacked her in the face with his beer bottle. I jumped at his movement. I went from being shocked to being scared. Blood gushed instantly out of my mom's nose and mouth. Calvin went for another swing, but my mom covered her face and started kicking wildly towards his waist. She connected a heel to his manhood. That's when Calvin doubled over and fell to the floor.

"Aghh, shit! Bitch!" he yelled.

My mom took advantage of him at his weakest moment. She scurried to her feet and kicked him in the stomach. I was scared, but I was starting to get excited. I thought the tables had finally turned and we were on top now. It was our turn to rid our lives of this demon. I ran over to help my mom by kicking Cal in the face. He pushed me back hard before I could even touch him. I flew back only to find the edge of a wooden desk cracking me in the back of my head. I felt like one of those cartoons when they get hit and that long pink knot grows out of their head. I was out of the game that quick.

After he knocked me down, he grabbed my mom by her ankle and yanked her to the floor. He crawled on top of her and started hitting whatever spots she didn't cover with her arms. He even hit those too! I couldn't think of anything else to do but scream. After a while there were loud knocks on the door. Calvin must've thought it was the police because he had a look of shock and fear on his face.

"Get yo ass in the bathroom! Hurry up!" he said to my mom.

She hurried to that bathroom too! Calvin tried to pull himself together before he answered the door.

"How may I help you?" he said to the people on the other side of the door.

"We heard screams and loud noises, sir. Is everything ok?" the person on the other side of the door asked.

"Yes, that was just me and my daughter playing. She hit her head, but she's ok."

I saw a white man peek in to look around. He also took a glance at me. I heard him say, "Sir, with all due respect and honesty, your room looks like a fuck hole. What's really going on?" He glanced around the room again and said, "You know what? I'm going to do you a favor. Leave now before I call the police. Just leave. I'll be back in five minutes. If you're not gone, you'll be going to jail."

Cal cleared his throat, "You got it. Thank you."

"No problem," the man said.

Calvin closed the door quickly but quietly. He gave me a hard look and yelled, "Get all yo stuff and put it in your backpack now! Theresa! Get on out here because it's time to go. We gotta move."

Cal felt like we weren't moving fast enough, so he started packing everything for us then rushed us out the door. It was late so it was kind of chilly outside. It was a bad time for Mother Theresa to try to start another argument. While we were riding in the car, my mom turned towards Cal with an evil glare on her face.

"So you ain't gone apologize for what you did to us?" she asked him.

"What I did? Shhhhi! You better off being quiet right now," he said.

My mom popped her mouth, "I see why she left you. You ain't no real man. You a little ass boy!"

"And you're a junkie bitch! Now shut the fuck up before I smack the shit outta you!" he yelled.

"You need to smack yo damn momma," Theresa said.

After that comment, Calvin gave her a hard stare. It was silent for a couple of minutes. My mom pulled out a bag of powder, dipped her pinky in it, and snorted it up her nose. She leaned back in her seat with her eyes closed. That's when Calvin pulled over at a corner.

"What I tell you about doing that shit in my car. Huh?" he asked in an angered voice.

"Nigga, fuck you…"

Before she could slur out the rest of her sentence Cal backhanded her. Therrrpppp! Then came slap after slap after slap.

"Get out! Now! Get out my car. You wanna be street trash, then I'ma put you in the street," Calvin preached.

My mom opened the door slowly. I guess she didn't move fast enough for Cal because he muffed her in the face and she stumbled out. He looked back at me and yelled, "Now what you gone do? You wanna stay with me or yo momma?"

My eyes were big as golf balls.

"Ummm, my mom," I mumbled.

"Then get yo ass out too," he barked.

My mom opened the back door and grabbed me and our bags. Then we started our journey walking down the cold street. My mom was sobbing and her face was bleeding. Her nose was busted and so was her mouth. She started to walk slower and slower until her knees gave out on her. She fell down to the sidewalk and cried for a couple of minutes. I just stood there with my hand on her back rubbing it and trying to comfort her the best way that I could.

"It's ok, Mommy," I reassured.

"I'm tired. I'm so tired, baby," she slurred.

She sobbed for a couple more minutes before she got back up. She looked horrible, and I felt broke down. It hurt me to see my mom like this and for us to have gone through what we did. I was only four, but I was holding on to emotions like I was 40 years old instead. My mom didn't have a cell phone, so we didn't call anybody. Who would she have called anyway? It seemed like all we had was Calvin until now. Once again, we were on our own and in the cold, heartless streets.

We veered off into the alleys, crossing from alley to alley until my mom finally broke all the way down. She dropped down on a big garbage bag like a sack of potatoes. I was shocked. I couldn't believe this was happening. I was cold, hungry, and the alley stank. It was dark and scary and everything was just horrible. What happened next was one of the events in my life that will always tear me apart when I think about it. I'm older now, and I really understand. We slept in a dark, nasty alley. We had gone from a house to a hotel to an alley. Fuck my life.

My mom started to sniffle, and told me to come here. She wanted to hold me, and I let her. I started to cry, and I couldn't stop. My nose was clogged, and my head hurt. I could feel my mom shivering. I didn't know where it came from but the question just came.

"Where's my dad, Mommy?" I asked.

"Baby, your dad's away in prison," she replied.

"Like on the TV?" I inquired.

"Yes, just like on the TV," she told me.

"Why he not on there then? Don't he wanna know me? I wanna see him," I complained.

"You will one day, Mami, you will. Now go to sleep," she said gently.

"I'm cold, Mommy," I said in a shivering voice.

"Get up," she said.

She reached in my backpack to pull out extra clothes and a jacket. She had me put on everything in there, so that I could stay warm. I don't know how, but I got cozy after a while. Soon after, fatigue took over my tiny body. I fell into a deep sleep as my mom cried into my hair. I thought I was dreaming when the sun came out and Calvin was right there in front of us.

"Theresa! Theresa, get yo ass up off the trash. You really slept in a alley with your daughter?" Calvin scolded.

"What?" My mom asked looking confused.

"Get yo dumb ass in the car," he demanded.

Once again Saint Theresa was under Cal's command. She gathered all our stuff to pack into his car. Every time I thought he was gone, he just came back. The next move was a much needed one because of our circumstances. Now we were moving into the devil's lair. She actually agreed to move in with that sorry bastard, the same one who had just abandoned us. My mom was beyond dumb, but she had to do what was needed. We were beyond desperate.

Chapter
04

Calvin stayed in a nice neighborhood. There were decorations in a lot of people's front yards. The grass was mowed, the sidewalks were clean, plus it was quiet. It was a place where you should've felt safe and peaceful, but that wasn't the case for me.

Things weren't so bad, at first. Well, at least they weren't that bad for me until Calvin's eleven year old son Roger moved in with us. His mom made him move in with Cal because he had behavior issues. But before he came, Cal gave us a heads up.

"Ok, ladies and babies," Cal announced when he walked through the door. "My son, Little Roger, is coming to live with us. His mom sicked him on us because she can't handle him. Can we get the job done?"

"Yeah!" I said aloud.

"You want a brother, Nani?" He asked.

"Yeah!" I replied.

"Ok then, go wash that little booty with those stinky feet so we can go pick him up," Cal requested.

"Yay!" I yelled excitedly before my mom pulled me off to the bathroom to get me ready.

We pulled up to an apartment complex with a brown skinned boy waiting with his long haired, tall mom. Those two were Calvin's son and ex-wife. Calvin got out to talk to her for a little bit. While they were talking, Roger ran towards the car with a smile on his face. He dressed nice and had a bunch of bags in his hands, including a big pack on his back. When Roger jumped in the backseat, my mom started talking to him. "How you doin' Roger? I'm Theresa, your dad's friend."

"Hi," he greeted.

"You happy to move back home?"

"Yeah," he answered then he looked at me. "Who's she? Your daughter?"

"Yup. Her name's Nani. Nani, say hi," Theresa said.

"Hi!" I said.

"Hi. You want some candy?" he asked me.

"Mmm hmm." I blushed.

"Nani, say thanks," my mom said.

"Thank you."

Calvin came back to the car, ready to leave. He looked in the backseat at Roger, "You ready to go, baby boy?"

"Yup," Roger said with a smile and a head nod.

I finally have a connection with someone, I thought. I had a make believe family now. I had a dad, a brother, plus my mom. I was starting to feel comfortable, and I almost forgot about the hell we had been through. I only come in contact with it in my dreams.

Cal's ex-wife was right. Little Roger was bad. He was always into something; he stole stuff whenever we went to the store, he cussed a lot, plus all he liked to do was play video games when he came home from school. I would always watch him play different types of games. He had everything from shooting games to sports games. Little Roger had it all. He always gave me stuff too. We were growing on each other, but one day all that changed. He came home from school with a movie instead of a game, but just like normal, he came home and played video games.

When my mom and Cal went off to some other part of the house, probably to go do drugs, he asked me if I wanted to watch a movie. Of course, I said yeah. He reached into his backpack to bring out a DVD with naked people on it, which I now know was a porno movie. He plopped the movie in and let it play for a little while. The image of what the people were doing wasn't unfamiliar to me due to Cal and my mom, but I felt weird and was attentive to the movie.

"You know what they doing?" Roger asked me.

"Yeah," I said.

"What?" he asked.

"Ummm," I had a confused look on my face because I realized that I actually didn't know the name of what they were doing. "I don't know," I continued.

"They doin' it. That's what they doin'," Roger said.

"It?" I repeated with a questioning look on my face.

"Yeah, girl. They doin' it. You know how to do it?" he asked me.

"No," I replied.

"You wanna learn?" he inquired.

"Uhhhh," I bellowed uncertainly, and before I could answer, he accepted the challenge for me.

"Im'a show you how," he said. "Take off yo pants and lay down."

I did. By that time, Little Roger was looking at the movie getting ready to imitate the man licking the woman's private parts. When he had studied long enough, he looked at me laying down with just my shirt on. He had a look in his eyes I hadn't seen before, a weird excited type look. The look made me excited too. I felt like this was an adventure. Some kind of grown up talent we could learn to be cool or something. The feelings that came over me after that were way off. I looked at him approach my private area with his face. Then he licked it. Then he licked some more. It felt wet, ticklish, and disgusting. It felt wrong. I felt like a million worms were crawling over me now. I quickly pushed Little Roger back. "Stop," I whined.

"What? Come on, Nani," he pleaded.

"No," I replied.

"Why you do that?" Roger asked.

"It feels nasty," I said.

He smacked his lips like he was impatient with me. "Man, come on," he said as he put a hand on my private area.

His hand felt even worse than his tongue. I felt so uncomfortable and protective of myself that I punched him in the face, "Stop! Leave me alone!" I cried.

"You little mutha…" He didn't finish his sentence, but everything seemed to pause.

He gave me a deep, vengeful stare. After a couple seconds, he turned off the TV and walked out the room. I put on my clothes feeling violated. It was one of the worst feelings of my life.

For days, I felt like there were bugs crawling all over me. The feeling was the worst in my private area. I didn't want anyone touching me there, not anyone. After that first time, I went to go find my mom. Guess what? Good ol' Saint Theresa was high out of her mind nodding in a corner with Cal close by, looking like a replica of her.

Even at a young age I knew not to waste my time even trying to talk to her while she was on drugs. I felt lost and alone. For the next couple of days I avoided Little Roger as much as possible. Every time I used the bathroom it felt funny and wrong. Every time my mom washed me I cringed on the inside. Every time I was around Little Roger I was uncomfortable. Dope Whore Theresa didn't notice any of it.

Me being a baby, I didn't know how to express it to her. All those feelings went away with time, but then everything went back to normal. It was like that moment with Roger never happened. I forgot about it, or should I say I forgot about how it made me feel until the second time it happened.

I was walking by Roger's room one day when I smelled something fruity. He was eating fruit snacks, the Scooby-Doo kind. They were one of my favorites. He had boxes of them. He probably stole them or one of his friends did. Who knows?

I stood in his door way with my mouth open. I was in awe of all those boxes of fruit snacks. I just knew he'd give me one.

"Roger, I want a box of the fruit snacks," I said.

"You want one of these?" he asked.

"Mmm hmm," I said as I nodded.

"Ok, What you gone give me? You gotta give me something," he said.

I shrugged my shoulders, "I don't know. Toys?" I said.

"I don't want no fuckin' little girl toys. I want a kiss!" Roger exclaimed.

"Ok," I agreed.

"Plus, we got to do it," he added.

"No." I responded quickly.

"Well, you can't have none. Get out my room," he said in a definite voice.

I stood there kind of upset that I couldn't get any, but after he snapped me out of it, I went on my way.

"Go! What you waiting on?" he yelled. That's when I turned around to leave.

He ended up suckering me in good with that candy. Later on that night I walked to his room. He offered me a pack of fruit snacks, but not a whole box. I took it too. That's when he asked, "You liked those? You want some more?"

"Mmm hmm," I murmured.

"You gotta do it with me," he said.

"I don't wanna do it," I said quietly.

"If you want my candy you do," he said.

There was silence for almost 5 seconds. I was thinking, but then I finally let "Ok," out of my mouth.

I can't believe I let him trick me like that for some fucking candy. Him and his no good dad got me with candy. I hate candy to this day.

He walked close up on me then tried to pull my pants down.

"No," I said.

"Just lay down."

I did.

"Get back up," he said.

I think he couldn't decide what he wanted to do.

"Just let me see it," he finally gestured.

"What?" I asked wondering what he was talking about.

"Yo private," he told me.

"Why?" I asked.

"You want this candy?" he asked again.

"Yeah," I said hesitantly.

"Then hurry up, and be quiet," was his response.

I undid my pants and started to pull them down. That's when he rushed in and pulled them down himself just so he could put his slimy little hand on my private and kiss me.

We both heard footsteps coming. My heart almost jumped right out my chest. I hurried up to pull my pants all the way up. Roger jetted to the other side of the room. When his dad walked in, Little Roger looked completely normal like nothing at all was going on.

"What y'all doin in here?" Cal asked.

"Nothing. She buggin' me about some candy," he told his dad.

Cal instructed, "Give her some candy then, Lil Nigga. Nani, you better be upstairs with yo mom in two minutes. Now hurry up."

Roger handed me a box of fruit snacks, and I quickly turned to go upstairs with my mom. I felt so icky and nasty that I didn't even eat that candy. I was feeling emotions I had never felt before, bad ones. They surely didn't have me feeling good at all, but the worst part was that I didn't even know why. I was confused, and already depressed at the age of four.

Little did I know then that it wouldn't be the last time Roger touched me. However, the last time Roger touched me was definitely his last time to touch me.

I was asleep in my bed one night with my mom, and I was lucky not to be alone. I was dreaming, and in my dream, a black snake was slowly crawling up my leg. I could feel it too. I was terrified. The snake started flicking its tongue at my private area. I went crazy trying to get it off of me. Then I suddenly woke up in a state of shock. I discovered the snake wasn't a snake; it was Roger. He was licking my womanhood while I was sleeping in my little panties. I screamed so loud and kicked so hard. I heard, "Aww, Shit!" as I connected with something.

"Little Roger what the hell you doing in here?" my mom asked in a shocked voice.

"Nothing," he whimpered.

"He was licking my private! He was doing it to me when I was sleep!" I screamed.

Roger started to stutter. Then my mom got red. It was dark, but I still could tell that Mother Theresa was on fire. My mom screamed out, "You little bastard!" right before she grabbed Roger by his neck. She kept a grip on him while she walked him over to where her belt was hanging on the bathroom door. She turned Roger around and started beating him everywhere on his body with that belt. He was screaming like I never heard anybody scream before. He deserved it too; my mom beat him for a couple minutes before Calvin came through my bedroom door.

"What the hell?" Cal said in shock and anger. "What the fuck you doing to my son!?"

Cal got to my mom in two strides. He grabbed her from the back and body slammed her. He stood on top of her then started hitting her in the face. Little Roger ran to a corner to ball up, and I just stood there with eyes big as golf balls, full of fear, watching it all. While Cal was beating my mom, she started yelling, "He molested my baby! He molested my baby!" over and over again.

When the words finally registered in Calvin's head he stopped. "What did you just say?" he asked.

"He molested Nani. He was messing with her while we was sleep, Calvin," my mom sobbed.

The whole scene looked so sad. Little Roger was in a corner looking like someone had a gun on him. Calvin was on top of a bloody-faced Theresa, looking like a crazy man. Poor me, I was on the bed looking like I just saw a corpse. My body was buzzing. Everything seemed to move in slow motion. I jumped when Cal started talking to me.

"Nani," Cal asked sternly. "Did Roger touch you?"

"Yeah," I said quietly.

"Where?" he asked.

"My private," I told him.

He then focused his attention on Roger. "Boy did you touch her?"

"No, no sir," Roger whimpered.

"So Theresa and Nani lying on you?" Cal asked Roger.

"YES," he answered his dad with a straight face.

I interrupted, "No, I'm not! He did it to me while I was sleeping! He licked my private!"

"No I didn't! I didn't!" Little Roger cried out.

Calvin wasn't going for it though. All of a sudden he leapt off of my mom and snatched Roger up. The fear in Roger's eyes was deeper than mine.

"You nasty lil nigga! I'ma beat yo ass! Take yo trifling ass in the room and be ready!" Cal yelled at him before throwing him across the room.

Roger got up so quick he looked like he was running from a monster. In all actuality he really was, but he didn't run to that room like he was supposed to. Instead, he tried to run away and out the door. I didn't see it, but that night when Roger ran out into the street he died. He got hit by a car. To this day, we still don't know who ran him over.

Even though Roger did something awful and gruesome to me, he didn't deserve to die. During that time in my life, a part of me died too. I could never be the same. I could never be the woman that I was supposed to be because of Little Roger and his evil dad. Those two traumatized me worse than anything I could have ever imagined, but it all started with Calvin.

Chapter
05

t's been a year since Roger's death. In between that time and when I turned five, things became more depressing. The drugs and liquor got worse. Calvin cut back on the heroin only to start messing with cocaine. He got drunk a lot too, pretty much every day. He was always grumpy and mean when he was hitting the juice. He even started beating on me.

Heroin still owned my mom.

At the age of five I thought my life couldn't get any worse, but on the one year anniversary of Roger's death, Cal showed me that I hadn't seen nothing yet. He became delusional. He even blamed me for Roger's death. And because I was so young, I felt guilty for it too. I just didn't know any better at the time. As I got older though, I realized that it wasn't my fault. It was his and his parents' fault. I didn't tell Roger to come molest me with his tongue in my sleep. I didn't tell him to try to run into the street instead of taking his just punishment. However, when I was four Calvin let me believe otherwise. You already know ol' Saint Theresa didn't do nothing to stop him either.

I remember everything clearly. It was late and raining outside. Calvin was in the living room drinking and looking at a picture of Roger. I was watching him from the bottom of the stairs. He must've seen me through the TV because it was kind of dark in the house. There was just a glow from a small lamp. I heard him sniffling. He was crying or maybe he had just stopped crying.

"Girl, what you doing? Spying on me?" Cal asked me out of nowhere.

My eyes got big as tennis balls.

"Hunh? Umm, nothing. I'm not spying on you," I said.

Calvin took a deep swig of his drink.

"Get yo ass over here. Ain't no telling what you might do. You might try to seduce and kill me next."

"I didn't mean to," I stated.

"Shut up!" he screamed. "Shut yo ass up! You smart? You smart, ain't you? You tryna be a woman like yo trifling ass momma?" he said, and then he paused like he was waiting for an answer. "Im'a show you how to be a woman like yo momma," he told me.

I looked at him like he was insane. I had fear written all over my face, and he lost it right then and there. Calvin palmed my face and shoved me to the ground. My heart dropped down to my belly. I was petrified. He grabbed me by my left leg and dragged me closer to him. Calvin started snatching off my shoes then reached for the top of my pants to pull them down. That's when I tried to defend myself. I gave him the hardest punch I could give, and it landed right on his nose.

"You little bitch! I can't believe you just hit me," he said as he straddled me with his big body.

It felt like an elephant was sitting on me. Cal reached back to smack me. That hit made me see white dots, and inside, my head was banging. He was screaming some-thing at me, but I was out of it. He unbuckled my pants. I felt so hopeless and helpless. I felt lost. I felt doomed. I wanted to scream, but I couldn't. I was discombobulated from that smack.

The life I was living and the things I went through made me want to die, but that time something saved me. It was a knock at the door. Calvin looked up kind of annoyed and startled. He grabbed me by the jaw.

"You keep yo ass quiet, you hear me? Go in that closet and don't make a peep. You bet not come back out until I say so. Now go!" he said.

I grabbed my shoes and rushed to that closet. I got inside and shut the door. I cuddled up in that dark corner like a wounded puppy. I had no type of hope in me. I started to cry, but I didn't dare make a noise. It was hard for me to breathe. I was hyperventilating a little bit, but I was still able to stay quiet. I could hear a woman's voice talking to Calvin. Come to find out, it was his ex-wife. I overheard some of the conversation while I was hiding in that tiny closet.

"Calvin, look at you. You're a mess. I know it hurts, I do, but we can get through this," his ex-wife said.

"How? What? What you gone say? Go to that floozy ass church? Go on with that!" he told her.

"Cal, please, please! Pastor Rick would love to see you there. Just try it out. It's helping me," she said.

"No!" he yelled.

I heard a long pause and then, "Well, if not for me then do it for Roger," she pleaded.

A couple seconds later, I heard the door shut. Then I heard Calvin's footsteps approaching the closet. My heart dropped again. I thought he was going to open the door, but he didn't. I waited in that closet for hours. I waited all night actually. I was cold, scared, and hungry. Every time I went to sleep I didn't even realize I had fallen asleep until I nodded and my head jerked back up. I even peed on myself.

It was Sunday morning when Cal opened the closet door. The light blinded me for a little bit, and I could barely stand up.

"Yo mom still ain't came back yet, so go wash up and get dressed. Eat you some cereal too. We going to church," he said.

I didn't even answer him. I was too afraid to do so. I just waited for him to walk off before I hurried to my room. I got some clothes, washed up, and ate as fast as I could before Calvin changed his mind. I really didn't feel like eating, so I just picked at my food. I was distraught, if that is even possible for a kid that age. I was just hoping that Calvin didn't come and jump on me again.

"Nani!" I heard Calvin yell out. It made me jump. "Come on girl. We gone."

That day was my first time ever, to my knowledge, of ever stepping foot in a church. There were a lot of people, and everyone was dressed nice. I felt beneath them. I felt like I didn't belong with them, but at the same time I felt comfortable. It was just me and Calvin together. We saw people of all types. We saw old, young, married, single, older kids, and babies. Everyone was singing and smiling. It seemed like everyone was happy.

A lot of people greeted me and Cal like we were old relatives at a family reunion. After that I ended up going to Sunday school with the other kids in the church. Calvin and I were separated and I liked that. I was beaming inside. I had a ball in Sunday school. I realized that I loved church. We had snacks while we talked and watched videos. Everyone just seemed so peaceful and happy; all because of God.

When I got a chance to marinate on that thought, it overwhelmed me. While at church, I heard God could deliver you from and help you with anything. Maybe it was true. It sure looked like he helped all those people in that church. I wonder if they've been through what I've been through. Maybe, maybe not, but who cares? All I know is that I wanted to be happy with God just like they were.

I finally had hope. At the church, they said all you had to do was ask and have faith. I just knew Roger would be alive again, my mom would get off drugs, and Calvin would finally get out of our lives. I prayed for that after church that night, but to no avail. None of that stuff ever happened.

The whole ride home neither one of us talked. We both had our own thoughts floating through our minds. By the time we got home we finally found out where my mom had been. She had been out selling her body to and for the dope man. As if that wasn't enough, she ran up a debt. At the time, her money trouble wasn't a big deal to me, but it was enough for the young guy to come into our home and start picking and choosing what he wanted.

When we walked into the house, my mom was crying. She was on her knees begging some young man. Calvin paused and was surprised just like me. The man looked at Cal for a couple of seconds before asking, "You her husband? 'Cause she owe me, and if I don't get my money, then I'm clearing this piece out."

Calvin gave the young man a snooty look and a smirk. "You ain't gone clear shit up in here. She..." Cal was interrupted by the man flashing a gun.

"Like I said, Te-te here owes me $1,500, so if I don't get it then I'm clearing this house out!" the man said.

"'Ey, look man, is it that serious that you gotta come up in my home and threaten me over $1,500?" Calvin asked calmly.

The man chuckled. "Yeah, it is. Once we got tired of her suckin' and fuckin' everybody, she ran up a bill. Somebody gotta pay it, and it ain't gone be me," the man told Calvin.

"I see. Look, man, you have my word that I'll get you the money. You swing by here tomorrow, and I'll take you to the bank in the morning."

The man paused, looked at my mom then back at Cal. "A'ight, bet. That's a deal," chuckled the man.

"A'ight," said Cal.

Everyone remained in their places until the man walked out the house, drove off, and disappeared from sight.

"Oh my God, oh my God. Calvin, thank..."

SLAP!!

Calvin slapped my mom before she could finish her sentence. It was one of the hardest slaps I ever heard. She looked rough already, but the slap made her look worse.

He didn't stop there though. He straddled her and started punching her in the face. Punch after punch after punch. She was turning into a bloody mess.

I think the punches hurt so much that she couldn't even scream. Cal ended up breaking her nose that night. Her face looked like a mask from that beating. After that, I was even more afraid of Calvin. He didn't even yell at her while he was hitting her. In my head, I couldn't even imagine what he could do to me. I was glued to my spot by the front door until Calvin snapped me out of it.

"Nani! Go to your room and don't come out until I tell you to," he demanded.

I didn't even give him a response. It wasn't necessary. I just jogged up to my room, shut the door, and jumped on my bed. I cried uncontrollably. My life was hell. That night was the first time I ever prayed. I reflected on all of my problems and I just let everything go. I believed God would help me just like they told me in Sunday school.

I got on my knees, put my elbows on my bed, and pressed my hands together.

"Dear God, my name is NaNida. I need your help. For years, this man named Calvin has been in me and my mom, Theresa's, lives. He beats on us and does drugs. He got my mom on drugs too. I just ask that you please get him out of our lives and make everything back to how it was before we met him. Please, get my mom off of drugs. Please, make her pretty again. Calvin has a son named Roger too. He died. He got hit by a car, and I feel like it's my fault. If you would, could you please bring him back into Calvin and his mom's life? In Jesus' name I pray. Amen."

Chapter
06

You'll never believe this one. The man that showed up at the house with my mom never got paid. He ended up going to jail the next day before he could even come to our house. When Calvin took my mom to the hospital they made a report on the dope man. They lied and said that he was the one who beat my mom's face in.

She stayed in the hospital for a couple days. Calvin didn't bother me in her time away either. Even though we hadn't been back to the church, I thought maybe the church had gotten to him too. I was wrong. A week after my mom came back home, so did the ways of the past.

Calvin and my mom were in the kitchen talking. Now, going back to church was on my mind, but I never asked Calvin because I was afraid to. I was afraid of the rejection. I wanted to wait for the right time to ask my mom so I wouldn't interrupt them. When I walked into the kitchen, they were staring at each other. Calvin took a big gulp from the bottle of liquor he was drinking. My mom had an evil scowl on her face.

"Mommy?" I said.

Saint Theresa turned her head slowly to me and smiled.

"What's up, Mami?"

"Ummm, when you were gone, Calvin took me to church," I said.

There was a pause. My mom turned and gave Cal a surprised glare. I continued.

"I want to go back. I want us to on Sunday."

"You want me to go too?" she asked.

"Yup," I said with a smile.

"Why?" my mom asked smiling as well.

"Because I want us to go as a family. I love you."

"I love you too, Mami," she replied.

Calvin scoffed. "You don't love shit but dope," he said.

"Calvin!" my mom said sternly.

"Bitch, she knows. She know what you is. You'll do anything for some boy." He paused then looked at me. "Nani, she'd sell you for some dope," he said with a smirk.

"Calvin, stop!" my mom exclaimed.

"Nah. The truth hurts, huh? Nani, yo mom will do anything, and I mean anything, for a hit of that dope. Do you know she..."

Before he could finish his sentence my mom punched him in the face. Calvin fell back on the floor. His liquor bottle fell and shattered. Theresa hopped up and went straight to the sink to grab a knife. Even though Cal was off balance when he got up, he still managed to do it quickly. My mom missed with the first swing of the knife. The second swing got her a fist to the face. She fell, and dropped the knife.

"You tried to stab me? You was gone stab me, bitch?" Calvin said before punching her again.

I stood there scared and in shock while I watched what was going on. Just like countless times before, Calvin was drunk and crazy. Theresa trying to stab him really touched a spot within him. It hurt him emotionally.

Cal started dragging my mom out of the kitchen screaming, "I'ma kill you! Bitch, I'ma kill you!"

"Ahhhh! Ahhhh! Let me go!" my mom screamed while kicking at Cal. "Nani, get help! Go! Get somebody!"

While my mom said this, I remained still. At that point, I wasn't going anywhere. Who did she expect me to go get? We didn't call the police. I just wasn't taught to do that. I didn't know any neighborhood people either. I didn't have friends with parents. The only place I could think of was the church, but I didn't know how to get there. I was stuck in my mind going through my options when Calvin picked my mom up and body slammed her. It knocked the wind out of her. Calvin started screaming in her face.

"Shut up! Shut! Up!"

That's when I started to run out the house to go get help. My mom looked desperate. After that slam, she was out of it. The wind hit my face. It was cold, and my cheeks felt like they were freezing. It was night time, so I was not surprised to see no traffic. I had a lot of energy back then, but even though I was running, I was getting nowhere. I didn't know where the church was or how to get there, but after 30 minutes of running and walking around, I found a church. It wasn't the place I was looking for, but it would have to do.

I walked up to the doors and tried to open them, but they were locked. I started to knock and, of course, there was no answer. I started to knock harder and scream out hello, but it was to no avail. I gave up after about five minutes or so then slumped down on the church steps. I was cold, and I wanted to go back home. The problem was that I didn't feel confident enough in myself to know that I knew how to get back home.

I started to feel like maybe that was a good thing because I didn't want to go back anyway. That house was hell. How could I have gone through all that crazy stuff by the age of five? This wasn't a life for me. I began to think about all the bad memories, the fights, the beatings, Roger, the drugs. It all just overwhelmed me, and I broke down and cried.

I didn't want to be me. I wanted to jump out of my body and go be someone else so bad. I turned to the church, got on my knees, and started to pray.

"Dear God, It's NaNida again. I tried to find the church so I could help my mom. Please make sure she's ok. Calvin beat her again. Please, please, please help us. Please," I prayed.

Through my eyelids I could tell there was a big white light behind me. For a second I thought it was God. My heart began to flutter, but I soon realized it was a car. My heart dropped when I heard Calvin's voice.

"Nani! Nani! Get yo ass in this car!"

I popped up scared, then slowly walked to the car. Calvin was back in the car by the time I opened up my door. When I sat down he backhanded me in the face. My nose started to burn, and there was a ringing noise in my head.

"Who the fuck told you to leave out the house? Huh?" he yelled.

SMACK!!

"Got me running around looking for you and shit!" he continued.

SMACK!!

"You lucky the police ain't get you. You bet not leave

out my house again unless you ready to stay out! You hear me?" he asked.

SMACK!!

My mouth and nose were bleeding now. I can't believe I was able to take the pain of that beating for that long. Eventually, I balled up. I should've done that from the beginning because he left me alone after that. That is, until we finally got back to the house. When we pulled up into the driveway, Calvin got out and slammed his door. He came to the passenger side and yanked the door open. He snatched me out like I was a grown woman. He pulled me inside the house by the arm. When we got into the living room, he told me to take off all my clothes and get into the tub with my mom.

I sobbed the whole way there. When I opened the bathroom door, my mom was naked in the tub. She was crying just like I was. She had a swollen eye and a busted nose and mouth. I could only imagine how I looked. When my mom looked up and saw me, she cried even harder. She put her arms out for me, and I rushed right into them. We cried together. That's when evil Calvin snatched me from the back of my shirt and flung me across the floor.

"Didn't I tell you to take them clothes off?"

"Ye-ye-yes," I stammered.

"Then do it! Hurry up!" Cal yelled out at me. "You betta have yo ass in that tub by the time I get back," he said before he walked out the room.

I rushed to get my pants and shirt off. I managed to get one sock off before I felt a belt slap me across the lower part of my back and butt.

"Ahhhhh!" I shrieked.

"Get yo ass in that tub!" he demanded.

I hopped painfully into the tub with my mom.

"Let me tell you two bitches something. We gone get some understandin' tonight." He looked at me directly in the eyes then pushed the belt in front of my face. "You bet not never leave this house again like that or interrupt grown folks conversation. What you thought you was doing?" he yelled.

"I was ju-ju-just tryin' ta-ta help," I cried.

"Shut up, trick!" he yelled. "And you," he said turning his attention to my mom. "You think I'm a game? You think you finna keep spendin' my inheritance money on dope? You think you gone keep goin' out for days on end suckin' and fuckin' the world then bring niggas up in my house 'cause you owe money, bitch?"

That's when he smacked my mom in the face with the belt. I jumped. My soul almost jumped out of my body. I was petrified. I thought Calvin was going to torture us or something.

My mom screamed. "Calvin, I'm sorry! I'm sorry! I'm sorry! I'm sorry!"

"Too late! You cost me my wife and my son. I should kill both you hoes. I should kill you right now."

"Calvin, please!" she pleaded.

"Shut up, Theresa," he said quietly.

I was frozen with fear. My heart was balled up in my chest, and I couldn't breathe. Calvin looked like a crazed mad man. He had already beaten us. Now, he wanted to kill us. Whatever pain he felt we caused him was his own fault, not ours. *He* came into *our* lives. We didn't come into his. He got my mom hooked on drugs. She didn't introduce him to heroin. His pervert son molested me. I didn't try to lick his private while he was asleep. He could have easily left us in that alley and got out of our lives. We would've eventually been ok.

Calvin filled the tub up with cold water. He made us sleep in it. Well, at least that's what he told us to do when he turned out the lights and left. My mom held me in her arms, sobbing, telling me it was gonna be ok. I tried to think, but I couldn't. My whole body hurt. That tub *was* torture. I was freezing and scared. We were shivering like Shaggy and Scooby in that tub, plus it was pitch black. It was like an Ice Hell. Once again, this was a moment where I didn't know how I managed to fall asleep, but I did.

When I started to dream, I was naked out in the snow; there was so much falling that it was almost like a blizzard. Then there was that black snake again. It was crawling towards me slowly. The snake was hissing Roger's name. I was trying to get away from it before it got too close, but I couldn't move. The snake just got closer and closer until it crawled up my feet past my legs and all the way up to my cheek. I smacked the snake off my face and screamed. That's when I woke up to see Calvin in the dark. I instantly thought more torture was coming. I couldn't tell if my mom was awake, but I'm pretty sure she was.

"Y'all get dressed. Breakfast is on the table. When you done eating Nani, go to yo bedroom. Don't come out unless I call you, or you gotta use it. Theresa, meet me in the room," he said.

Then Cal splashed us in the face with water before he turned the light on and left out the bathroom.

It felt like the light had stabbed me in my eyes. When we tried to get out of the tub, we realized that it wasn't going to be easy. I don't know about my mom, but my legs had fallen asleep and were wobbly. I had to crawl out. She was weak too, but she managed a lot better than I did. She helped me up, took me to my room, and dressed both of us without saying a word. All of that happened just because I asked to go to church as a family, but worse than that, we had still never gone.

Chapter

07

i was to start school soon and was excited about it. I experienced heaven and hell when I first started going. The torture got worse, but eventually, I met an angel.

I remember my first day in Ms. Hill's Nine Rivers kindergarten class. It was magical in a way. I got to hang around a lot of other kids my age, and all the adults that helped out were nice and sweet. We played games. We ate snacks. School was fun. I felt like it was my safe haven.

On my first day in class, I walked into a big classroom with children everywhere. Some were smiling, some were laughing, and some had a nervous look on their faces, like I'm sure I did. Some were even crying.

The classroom was beautiful. It was colorful. There were pictures on the wall of animals and bugs. There were pictures of the ABC's going around the room including pictures of objects to help us remember the letters. You know, like A for apple, B for ball, and C for cat.

I liked the race car mats on the floor too. I can't forget about all the toys that were in the corner in the back. But my favorite thing about that classroom was the view it had. It had 4 big windows overlooking the playground. And when Ms. Hill opened them, you could feel the nice warm, breezy air. You could also hear the joyous sounds of kids playing, laughing, and screaming, and an occasional cry or two because somebody had fallen and hurt themselves.

I walked around the classroom until Ms. Hill shouted, "Boys and girls find your desk with your name tag on it. Then wait for more instructions."

I found a big school-themed name tag that had NaNida written on it real neatly. I may not have known how to say my ABC's all the way through. I may not have been able to count all the way to 100 without messing up, but I sure knew how to spell my name.

After everybody was seated, a thin, pretty, white woman with long goldish brown hair said, "Hi, everybody. I'm your teacher, Ms. Hill. This is my first year teaching, and this is your first year in school. I know most of you don't have backpacks, and some of you may not have gotten your supply lists yet, but that's okay. My fiancé is a pastor of a church and the church has donated new backpacks and school supplies for all of you. So, let's get it all passed out, shall we?"

The mention of backpack made me want to throw mine away. It was old, stinky, and ugly. I definitely got me a new red backpack that day. The mention of church got me excited too. The thought came to my head that maybe I could go to church with Ms. Hill.

After everybody had gotten their supplies, we went to lunch, and then we went to recess. Finally, we watched a movie. That was the only year during my time so far going to school that the teacher didn't have everyone introduce themselves to each other on the first day.

When I came in the house from school my mom was sitting in front of the TV eating cereal. "How was school, Mami?" she asked me.

A big smile grew on my face. "It was fun. I got a new backpack and some crayons, markers, a lot of stuff," I responded.

"A lot of stuff, huh? Well, that's good, baby," she said.

"We watched a movie, too. Did you know we got toys in our classroom?" I asked excitedly.

My mom put on a fake dramatic face for my benefit. "Oh, you do? What kind?" she asked.

I had to think for a second. "Well, I guess dolls and stuff you can hold," I said with a smile.

"Any homework?" she inquired.

"Homework?" I replied.

"Your teacher didn't say anything about homework?" mom asked.

"No. Nothing," I said.

"Well, go on and make you a sandwich or something, then when you done, come cuddle up and watch TV with Mami," Mom said in a very relaxed tone.

Calvin picked me up from school that day and never once inquired about my day. He barely looked at me. Maybe that had something to do with Roger. Or maybe he was depressed. Or maybe he could've been fearful of the school finding out what he had been doing to me—like they did the next day.

Everything in class was mostly the same up until the point where everybody had to introduce themselves and tell everyone their favorite thing to do with their family. When it was my turn, I grew even more nervous than I was before.

"Hi, everybody. Umm, my name is NaNida Vasquez. Ummm. I don't really have a family like most people do. Well, I do, but I don't have a dad. Me and my mom don't do much. I like church. I only went once with my step-dad, though. Umm, that's all," I said nervously. I sat down, feeling beneath everybody again, like I did when we were at the church.

All the other kids had families. They all had aunts, uncles, brothers, sisters, grandparents, moms, and dads. You name it; they had it, but not Nani. I felt alone.

Right before lunch Ms. Hill asked me to stay in the classroom and eat with her. I was curious, nervous, and happy all at the same time. I was wondering *What could she want with me? What was so important or special about me that she wanted me to eat lunch with her?*

Ms. Hill had some leftover pizza she shared with me. It was good, too. We chit-chatted and laughed for a little bit, then she got around to what she really wanted to talk about.

"NaNida, I wanted to ask you about church and your family," Ms. Hill stated to me.

"Ok," I said.

"You seem a little nervous or embarrassed." She let the statement kind of hang in the air. "True?" she asked.

"True," I replied.

"Do you like church a lot?" she asked.

"Yeah, I do," I told her.

"What church did your step-dad take you to?"

"I don't know the name of it. I want to go back, but I'm afraid to ask again," I said in an uncertain voice.

A weird, questioning look grew on her face. "Afraid? Why would you be afraid to ask about church?" she asked me.

I started to feel awkward. "Ummm, last time I asked, my step-dad and mom had a big argument," I replied.

Ms. Hill started thinking—probably about her response. "Well, would you like to come to church with me next weekend?" she asked.

"Yes," I said with a smile on my face.

"One more question. I need you to be honest with me. Did your step- father hit your mom when they argued?" she probed.

At that question I tensed up. I froze. Right before I was going to answer, Ms. Hill said, "Tell the truth, NaNida. You won't be in trouble," she assured me.

"Yeah, he did," I mumbled.

"Did he hit you?" she asked.

"Yes," I answered quietly. Then the bell rang for recess. "Can I go play?" I asked.

"Yes, yes, go have fun," she told me. When I was just about to walk out of the door, Ms. Hill said, "Thanks for eating lunch with me, NaNida."

I looked back at her and said, "Welcome." I turned and walked out the door. The rest of the school day was kind of awkward for me because of the questions Ms. Hill had asked me.

It was the same silent routine when Cal came to pick me up, but he wasn't silent when he found out what Ms. Hill and I had talked about at school.

"So how was school, Sugar Mama?" Calvin asked me as he walked into my room.

I looked at him kind of surprised and curious. "Umm, it was good," I answered.

"That's good. Your teacher called today. You must've talked to her about church," he said cunningly.

My heart dropped. I could see the evil, angry look in his eyes. I didn't say anything to him. I just stared at him. The more silent I was, the more his anger rose.

"Why is she callin' here askin' questions?" Calvin screamed. "What did you tell her? You told her I hit you?" he asked.

I shook my head furiously, and then answered, "No. No. I didn't tell her nothin'."

"You did! Stop lying. What'd you tell her?" he yelled.

"Nothing," I said quietly.

"Don't make me smack you. I'ma ask you one more time. What did you tell her?" he asked, pausing after every word.

I took a deep breath before I answered, "I told her that you and my mom argued about church. She asked if you hit us and I said 'yeah,'" I told him trembling.

Calvin looked at me in silence. It was like he was studying or calculating me for an attack. Kind of like a lion or a tiger will do as they look at a herd of antelope. Just like the predator he reminded me of, he leaped at me out of nowhere and snatched me up by my shirt.

"You want me to go to jail? Huh?" he asked.

"No," I said in fear.

"Yes, you do. You think you smarter than me? I got something for you," he said.

He threw me on my bed and went into my closet look- ing for something. He had come out with the iron. He plugged it up then turned the heat level on it all the way up. "Take off yo clothes," he said quietly but sinisterly. "Hurry up," he said.

The way he said it put more fear in me than his yell. I took off all my clothes except my panties. I stood there shaking. I was terrified of what he was going to do. We stared each other down. He had a look of evil on his face; I had fear on mine.

Calvin unplugged the iron. I was frozen to the spot where I stood. I wish I could've run. He came to me in 3 long strides, but they seemed slow. Maybe everything was moving in slow motion at that time. He grabbed me by my left arm.

"You wanna tell shit?" he whispered to me. "I guarantee, you bet not tell this. If you tell that teacher or anybody else anything, I'ma kill you *and* them."

I believed him too.

He lifted me with ease by my arm and tossed me on the bed. Calvin straddled me, sitting on my back, burning my thighs with the iron. He kept taking the iron off and putting it back on my body. I might've screamed my ear drums out.

"Ahhhhh! Ahh! I'm sorry!" I screamed.

"Shut up! Shut up!" he yelled.

I continued screaming.

This went on forever in my mind. It couldn't end quickly enough. It felt like my skin was burning off of my thighs. When he was done burning me, I lay there crying and screaming. I thought I was going to die. I never wanted to see an iron, Calvin, or Ms. Hill again ever. When I finally opened my eyes, Calvin was getting ready to open my door to leave out of my room. He looked at me deeply. "If you think that was something, you betta times that by a thousand because if that teacher or anybody else questions me about my house again, I'ma kill you. I'ma torture you," he said. Then he walked out.

When he was gone, I could see my mom in the doorway with her hands to her face, crying. She knew. She knew what he was doing to me and she let him do it. Cal could've done anything he wanted to me and she would've just let him.

I didn't go to school for almost a week. When I finally went back to Nine Rivers I could tell Ms. Hill was distressed. But she held it in all the way up to lunch time. She approached me like I was a regular kindergartner. I wasn't, though. I was far from being a normal little girl my age; I had been exposed to too much.

"NaNida," Ms. Hill said in a baby voice. "I didn't see you at church. I thought you wanted to come with me," she said.

"I do," I said with a shy smile.

"I talked to your mother. She said she would bring you," Ms. Hill stated.

"She doesn't have a car," was my excuse.

She paused for a second. "Is everything ok? We haven't seen you for a while. Were you sick?" she asked.

I shook my head. "No."

"Well, go on to lunch. I just wanted to make sure everything was fine with you," she told me.

When she was finished, I turned around slowly and silently walked to lunch.

I didn't do anything at recess but sit on the swing by myself. When we came back in from outside, Ms. Hill introduced me to some other lady and she took me into a back room inside the office.

The lady was a plump, brown-skinned black woman. She looked more like a principle than some kind of counselor. "Hi, NaNida. I'm Mrs. Anderson," she said to me.

"Hi," I replied back.

"Take a seat and get comfortable. You're not in trouble or anything. It's been brought to my attention that you missed a lot of days of school. I just want to ask you a couple of questions to make sure that you are alright."

"Ok," I mumbled.

"So, is everything ok at home? Were you sick?"

A memory flashed of Calvin with that iron, and the threat he had made. "I'm ok and wasn't that sick. But I'm all the way ok now," I told her.

"Ok, that's good you're alright now, NaNida," Mrs. Anderson said with a smile on her face. "I want to make sure you're ok in the future, too."

She let the statement hang in the air for a little bit. I didn't give her any type of response. I was nervous and ready to leave, but at the same time, I wanted to stay. I didn't want to go back home. I didn't want to get tortured again because these people were asking questions.

"I'll be ok in the future too," I said when I caught the hint that she wanted me to say something.

"Well, will you promise me that if anything goes wrong like you being sick or someone hitting or touching you, that you will tell an adult?" she asked.

"Yes," I replied.

"Has anyone ever hit you, NaNida?" she asked as she studied me.

"No, ma'am," I told her.

"Ok, promise me you will let me know if you're in danger or anything. We care about you," Mrs. Anderson assured me.

"Thank you, ma'am," I said.

"Go back to your class now," she told me.

I smiled, and then walked to Ms. Hill's class slowly.

The rest of the day went by slowly, but too fast for me. I hoped that the lady asking me questions didn't get back to Cal. Thankfully, it never did.

I was really surprised when I saw my mom waiting for me as I walked outside of the school, instead of Calvin.

"Hey, baby!" my mom said with a smile on her face.

"What happened? Where's Calvin?" I asked.

"The car broke down. We're gonna take the bus, but we gotta set you up for the school bus now. So come show me where the office is."

I grabbed my mom's hand and walked her through the other students and teachers into the office.

"Hi, I need to know who I need to talk to about getting my daughter assigned to a school bus. Our car broke down," my mom said to the secretary. She never got a chance to respond because the lady I talked to earlier spoke up.

"Ms. Vasquez?" Mrs. Anderson asked.

"Yes," Mom said.

"You're trying to get NaNida on a school bus?" she asked.

"Yes, ma'am." my mom replied.

"Come in my office, please," invited Mrs. Anderson.

"Ok. Thank you. Wait out here, Mami," my mom said to me.

Good ol' Saint Theresa talked to that woman for almost an hour. At least, that's what it felt like. I don't know what they talked about. More than likely it was about me and Calvin. We'll never know. But that next day was my first day on a school bus. That's when I met my angel. He always stood up for me and protected me. His name was Danny, Danny Rogers. Imagine that.

Chapter
08

ood ol' Danny Rogers, the preacher's son. My first day on the bus was when I met Danny. He stopped a couple of boys from picking on me. Danny was older; he was in the 4th grade. I never thought it was odd having a white boy take up for me, but some people did.

My mom got me up earlier than usual to get me ready for school. Even though Calvin had the money, I didn't dress as nice as all the other kids. My long hair was in a raggedy, puffy pony tail. My shoes were dusty just like my outfit. They weren't dusty like covered in dust; they were dusty as in worn and just plain old. You sure could tell it wasn't new.

When I was finally ready for school, my mom walked me down to the bus stop on the corner of our block. There were two other kids that were with their mom or dad, and there were three older kids that were alone. By older I mean third graders.

We waited for about ten minutes until the bus finally came. I was nervous and excited at the same time. I wanted to be around a lot of other kids, but I was also afraid of what they'd think of me.

I had an old black man for a bus driver. He dressed in a plaid button up shirt and wore a dusty old hat (it really did have dust on it). He looked at me and said in a deep voice, "Your seat is in the back on the right hand side. You'll see your name tag."

I looked at all the other kids. They were of all ages and races. Some of them looked way too big to be on the bus. I proceeded to walk through them and found my name tag. My seat was the third from the last.

I sat next to an Asian girl. She was older than me. Therefore, she didn't pay me too much attention. She probably thought she was "cooler" than me. She was busy playing games or texting on her cellphone from what I could see.

I sat next to her in silence and peace until I felt something hit the back of my neck. I looked back and didn't notice anything out of the normal, but when I turned back around I heard snickering. It happened again. I didn't look back that time. Whoever had done it waited a couple of seconds longer then did it again.

"Leave me alone. Stop messing with me," I looked back and said.

"Shut up, little girl. Ain't nobody messing with you," a chubby, freckle-faced white kid said.

I slouched down in my seat hoping whoever it was throwing stuff at me couldn't hit me anymore, but it didn't work. They still managed to pick on me. Next thing I knew, somebody pulled my pony tail. I flung my arms back without looking, trying to swat whoever it was. I guess I looked crazy because a lot of kids in the back started laughing. I didn't want to, but I couldn't help it; I started to cry.

"Can you please stop messing with me?" I asked no one in particular.

"Awwww. It's ok little cry baby," the freckle faced kid said.

"Cry baby, cry baby, cry baby," some boys started chanting.

That just made me cry even more. Then a mixed boy that was sitting next to Freckle Face got up out of his seat and started pushing me. He was laughing like I was some type of toy to play with or something. I swung and hit him in the face. That's when he grabbed me. That's also when Danny grabbed him and slammed him into his seat. Danny held the boy in a headlock.

"You wanna fight, Troy? Huh? Fight me and stop pickin' on little babies," Danny said to him.

"I'm sorry. I'm sorry, Danny," the boy panted.

"Go back to your seat and leave her alone," my hero said as he pushed the boy into the aisle. "Scott! You freckle faced punk! I'm kickin' your ass after school for starting this."

"You don't even know her!" Scott said.

"God don't like bullies. Just say you're sorry to her, and I'll leave you alone," Danny demanded.

Scott looked at me and said, "Sorry for teasing you and messing with you. It was just a joke because you're new. Sorry."

I looked at him with tears in my eyes.

"Hey! Come sit with me," Danny said.

I got up and sat next to him. Danny was a husky and tall fourth grader. He was the best player on the basketball team, he was the biggest in the school, and he was Mrs. Rogers' son. From that moment on, Danny became my big brother and my best friend.

Ms. Hill had gotten married over the summer, so she became Mrs. Rogers. The Rogers became my second family. I went to church with them and slept over at their house on some weekends. Danny looked after me. He taught me things, played games with me, read the Bible to me, and everything. The Rogers were a blessing to me, especially Danny. He never once tried to touch me in the wrong way or anything. His father never yelled at us or hit us. They showed me a different way of life.

Danny was the reason I got baptized in the first grade. I'm blessed to have had him in my life. I love Danny. I love him so much; I don't think he'll ever know how much I cherish him.

Here is the story of my baptism. Saturday night, I was at home with Cal, and my mom was out somewhere getting high. She had already gotten my Sunday outfit ready before she disappeared on one of her escapades. I was in my room reading a book when Cal busted in. I could tell he was drunk even though he wasn't carrying a bottle around like he usually did when he was drinking. His eyes were bloodshot, so he was probably high too. He pulled the cigarette he was smoking out of his mouth to ask me a question.

"When them honkies comin' to pick you up?" he asked with an evil stare.

I gave him an innocent yet hard stare. I knew what he meant, but I wouldn't respond to it because I cared about these people, and they treated me better than he did.

"You hear me, girl? I asked you when them damn people comin' to pick you up," Cal yelled.

"They're not damn people or honkies. They're the Rogers family."

"What?" Calvin asked me with his face balled up.

I realized then that I had pushed a button.

"They'll be here in the morning," I hurriedly added on.

"Naw, naw, naw, naw. You tried to hit me with that smart alec shit again. What I tell you about disrespecting me, girl?" he asked.

"I didn't disrespect you," I replied with remorse.

"Naw, naw. Yes, ya did" he chuckled with an evil grin.

That's when he came over to me and looked down on me for a minute. It felt like my heart was beating out of my chest. He was drunk and we were alone, plus he had a lit cigarette. There was no telling what he had on his mind. He finally let out a response.

With a smirk on his face he said, "You're lucky." Then he lashed out and grabbed me by my throat. He whispered into my ear, "You lucky I don't feel like beatin' yo ass tonight, but if you ever, ever disrespect me like that again, it's gone be the last of you. I'm tired of yo snobby little ass. You ain't white." Then he roughly turned me around, lifted up my shirt and put the cigarette out on my back.

I screamed out in pain, but he pushed my face to the floor to muffle my cries. His rage for the moment all used up, he got up and left me alone in my room. I cried into that floor until I went to sleep. I wished my life was just a dream and that I could wake up to find out that none of the bad things in it had ever existed.

I woke up Sunday morning and went downstairs to find Calvin sleeping like he was in a coma on the couch. I wanted to burn him just to show him how it felt. I was thankful he wasn't awake and that I was able to get ready in peace. I knew that even if I did summon up enough courage to burn him, he'd just wake up and torture me.

I took a bath, ate breakfast, and got ready to put my Sunday clothes on. Just like the moment when I first took off my clothes to take a bath, I kept finger tracing my scars from the iron and the new burn on the lower part of my back. I wanted to cry, but I managed to hold it in. To be so young, I was very mature and strong-minded. Maybe it was because of my life and my struggle, but I felt like an old soul. I felt like I'd been here before. I finally got everything on and sat on the front porch as I waited for Mrs. Rogers and Danny.

When I saw their car pulling up, a big smile spread across my face. Nani was gone. I was NaNida when I was with them. I was in a completely different mindset. When we pulled into the church parking lot, I grew more excited than usual. I loved going to church. Being there with those happy people helped me in so many different ways. I got to get away from Calvin for one thing. I got to be around good people and be happy myself for a change. I felt safe, and it always kept my hope alive that one day things would be better for me.

When we walked inside the church, it was the same as always. People were smiling, laughing, and praising God. I was doing the same. I felt like I was in heaven. After the singing was all over, the younger kids split from the adults and went to Sunday school. When we came back, Mr. Rogers was introducing visitors and talking about new beginnings. Then he asked if anyone would like to be saved.

Danny nudged me and asked, "You saved NaNida?"

"I don't know," I replied.

"If you don't know then the answer is no. You ever been baptized?" he asked.

"What's baptized mean?" I asked him.

"You don't know?" he asked with surprise.

"I don't remember," was my reply.

"You gotta get baptized. My dad's gonna dunk your head into that fancy tub full of water," he said.

"In my dress?" I asked.

Danny looked at me with a smile and said, "No, silly."

"Naked?" I returned, starting to get nervous.

Danny laughed at that. He smacked his lips and said, "No, they'll give you a robe."

That's when Mr. Rogers asked, "Would anyone like to be baptized? It's never too late."

"You do," Danny whispered to me.

"No, I don't," I whispered back.

"If you want to go to Heaven you do. You do want to go to Heaven, don't you?" he asked me.

"I do," I said.

"So go," he told me.

"No," I told him with timidity.

"Yes!" he demanded.

I thought about it for a second.

"Ok, but only if you go with me," I said to him.

"We want to get baptized!" he yelled.

Then he grabbed my hand and stood up with me. I became nervous. There were a lot of people in that church. There were hundreds maybe, but it looked like thousands to my eyes. All of those people were now focused on me and Danny. As long as he was with me though, I was alright.

"Come on up here young man and young lady." Mr. Rogers said to us. "This is a blessing church! It's never too early for new beginnings with God either!" he said to the crowd.

Some men in suits escorted us down the middle aisle to the front of the church where Mr. Rogers was standing.

"Do you want to give your life to Christ and have Him guide you, son?" he asked.

"Yes, sir," Danny replied.

Then Mr. Rogers looked at me and said, "And you young lady?"

"Yes," I answered him.

Mr. Rogers's smile grew even bigger than it was before. "Do you want to get baptized?" he questioned.

"Yes," we said together.

"Well, follow these two gentlemen right here so they can get you ready for your new beginning in Christ," he said as he pointed to the two men that had escorted us from our seats.

They took us to a back room right behind the altar. They handed us each a purple and gold robe and led us to separate rooms to get dressed. As soon as I put on that robe, I felt important.

"You look nice, young lady," one of the men said to me.

I gave him a big smile. Hopefully he could read the thanks in my face because I couldn't say it verbally. Danny came out and smiled at me.

"You ready?" he asked.

I nodded my head with the same smile I had given the man. Danny took my hand into his and we made our journey up those back steps and up to the altar with his father. The crowd was singing and clapping. There was a very positive energy in the air. It all felt good and right. I placed my eyes on that fancy marble and gold tub. It looked like it was filled with crystal water. It was magical. All those people were smiling at us. It felt like they were cheering us on. It felt like we were famous singers or something.

Mr. Rogers was saying something to me, but I was so out of it that I didn't hear him. I didn't really know what he was saying. It was like I knew what he was saying because my body and brain reacted to it, but it was like my spirit just wasn't catching it. I know I stepped into the tub with Danny right by my side. The water was freezing cold, but I was having something like an out of body experience, so I didn't shy away from it or react like I normally would.

Danny went down in the water first. Then it was my turn. I remember Mr. Rogers asked me a few questions. I nodded my head and went under the water. I know realistically I was only under the water for about a second or two, but it felt like much longer. In that beautiful, magical moment of being under the water, all my worries, fears, and troubles seemed to have been washed away. The whole thing was spectacular. It was breathtaking. I felt new and really alive for the first time in my life. I felt free. When I finally came up, it seemed like I had just gotten back into my body.

"Welcome to Christ," Mr. Rogers said to me.

The whole church was clapping and cheering. Some people were even taking pictures. I swear I will never forget that moment. But there are a lot of moments with Danny that I will never forget. Like the time he taught me to ride a bike, or the time he told me about his girlfriend, Crystal Miller, and their first kiss. I most definitely won't forget the moment on my eleventh birthday when I told him about Calvin beating on me, amongst other things. By that time we were very close. We were like real brother and sister. I was actually surprised that I didn't tell him sooner. He cried when I told him about it all. He felt my pain.

It was a late night on the beach. There were kids running around in the sand with sparklers and people sitting around bonfires. Danny and I were lying in the sand next to each other, isolated from everyone else.

"How'd you like your party?" he asked me.

"It was wonderful. Best party I ever had, hands down," I said.

"Ever?" he asked.

"Ever," I said.

He smiled. "That's good. What made it the best?" he inquired.

I reflected on that question for a little bit before I answered. Pain came to me momentarily.

"Well, there were no drugs, no liquor, and no Calvin," I told him.

"WHAT?" he asked in surprise.

"Yeah, I had some wild times, dude," I said like a stoner.

"You're only eleven years old. You did drugs before?" he questioned.

"No, stupid! My mom and Calvin did. You already know about my mom, but my stepdad is the same. He's worse actually," I went on.

There was a brief silence before Danny asked, "Can I tell you something?"

"What is it?" I asked.

"Me and my dad noticed those marks. He didn't want to bring it up then. He didn't want to spoil your big day."

I looked at him and said, "That's good."

"How'd you get 'em?" Danny asked.

"Calvin," I told him.

Danny shook his head with his eyes closed.

"What did he burn you with?" he asked.

"An iron and a cigarette," I answered him.

"WHAT?" Danny shook his head in amazement. "And you never told anyone? Why?" he questioned.

"He said if I ever told anyone then he would kill me and whoever I told," I replied.

"You serious, NaNida?" Danny continued.

"Danny, you know I don't lie," I said.

There was silence for a couple of minutes. During that silence, I reflected on all of the things Calvin had done to me. I started to cry. My old demons returned for the first time since the day I got baptized.

"What else did he do?" he asked suddenly.

With tears in my eyes I answered, "He made my life a living hell. He took my mom away from me. It's all his fault that she's on drugs. I bet he thinks I don't know or don't remember, but I do. He beats me, burns me, and touches me!" I had to pause because I was too overwhelmed. I needed to release all that anger.

"We slept in an alley before because of him! I seen him shoot dope into my mom before too! He ruined my life. He ruined my life, Danny," I cried.

By then he was holding me in his arms swaying with me. He cried with me. He felt my pain, but he could never share my true torture. Never.

"It's ok. It'll be ok. We'll get 'em! We'll get 'em one day, I promise," he told me.

We never did "get" Calvin, but Danny did manage to stay by my side. I needed him then more than I ever needed anyone else before because the day after my party on that beach, my mom was found dead with a needle in her arm. I couldn't grasp it. My mom, dead? And from drugs? No, there was no possible way that was true. I couldn't—and wouldn't— accept it.

Chapter
09

he moment I finally accepted my mom's death was on the day of her funeral. I was staying with the Rogers family while they helped Calvin handle the funeral arrangements and get everything together. Mr. Rogers was nice enough to allow the funeral to be held at his church.

Calvin came over that morning to attend the service with us. I didn't really want to be around him, but as much as I may have disliked him, he was a part of my mom's life. I guess that he had a right to be there even though I felt like this whole thing was his fault in the first place. We all sat in the living room and waited for the limo to show up, and I started off into space thinking my own thoughts. I didn't speak to anyone. I mean, I really didn't want to.

Danny came over to me while I was sitting in the corner and asked if I was ok. I told him I couldn't be better. He looked down at me and cleared his throat before responding that he knew that Calvin being there bothered me and that he wouldn't let him do anything to hurt me.

"It's all his fault," I said, holding back tears.

"I'm here for you if you need me," he comforted.

I stared at him with an attitude. He didn't have anything to do with my anger, but he was around for me to release some of it anyway. We always seem to hurt those closest to us.

"Just leave me alone and let me be. I don't really wanna talk right now," I complained.

Danny touched my shoulder sympathetically and walked off. As time was getting closer for the limo to come, we all gathered outside to wait. Danny and I stood next to each other in silence. Calvin stood with Mr. Rogers.

"You holding up pretty well, Calvin?" I heard Mr. Rogers ask him.

Calvin looked at him slowly then said, "Yeah, of course. I know she's better off now, but it's still hard."

"I know. Death can be tough. I lost my father a couple years back," Mr. Rogers said.

Calvin put on a sad smile and said, "I lost my father about a decade ago. I lost my son as well."

He looked over towards Danny and me as he said it. He noticed me eyeing him.

"Sorry to hear that," Mr. Rogers said. "It would crush me to lose my wife and child. I can't imagine how you feel. NaNida's a tough camper though. You'll take care of each other, I'm sure."

"Got to," Calvin said before looking back at me. "You know we rented a nice limo, Sugar Mama?" he asked me.

I didn't say anything, but just looked at him in stern silence. I didn't know who rented the limo, nor did I care. It finally pulled up after a few minutes, and we all jumped in. It was real fancy on the inside. It had a mini bar, TV's, and fancy little colorful lights, but I didn't care too much about that at the moment. My thoughts were somewhere else. I was thinking that this would be the last day I ever got to see Saint Theresa ever again. It didn't help that the man I felt was responsible for her death was in the limo with us. At the same time though, it was like he was never there because I just stared down at my feet for ninety percent of the ride trying to block out reality.

When we pulled into the church parking lot there were a few cars already there. We all stepped out of the limo one by one. I was the last one out. Everyone that was there got out of their car and formed a line to walk into the church so the service could get started. I was the first one in line and the first one to see my mom in her casket.

When I looked down into that wooden casket, I saw a beautiful but ghostly looking woman. I saw Theresa Vasquez. A smile spread across my face as I pictured her laughing and playing with me. That's when I broke down and cried. I fell to my knees. I just couldn't believe it. The only blood relative I had left in my life was gone just like that, and on my birthday at that. I had no one— all because of drugs. All because of some stupid ass heroin.

Danny came to my side and held me for a while. While I let my sorrow loose, he helped me up and took me to sit in the front row. Danny held me while he whispered in my ear that he was with me and it was going to be ok.

"She's gone!" I sobbed.

Danny squeezed me tighter.

"I can't believe she's really gone," I said.

I kept on crying, and after a few minutes, I began to calm down a little bit. Although I was crying, I was watching the people who came to my mom's funeral. I saw a couple of obvious drug users, some supportive people from the church, and I even saw my mom's friend, Rhonda. Rhonda was the one who had duped my Mom when she had sold her the food stamp card with barely any money on it. I saw a man who I had never seen before, and he definitely wasn't a junkie. He looked too nice. He had heavy tears in his eyes like he had a lot of love for my mom too. Maybe he was her drug dealer or something. He was also staring at me throughout the funeral. I nudged Danny.

"You see that man?" I asked.

"What man?" he replied.

"That man in the brown. He keeps looking at me," I said.

"He probably knew your mom. Don't stress about him," Danny told me.

"Did he get invited?" I questioned.

"You don't invite people to funerals. It's public knowledge. Stop looking at everybody and pay attention," Danny advised me.

I rolled my eyes and fell in line with the funeral service. The service was as nice as it could've been, I guess. Mr. Rogers said some things and preached a little bit. Calvin even gave an emotional speech, surprisingly. If you had heard it you would've thought he was madly in love with my mom. One of my mom's heroin addict friends said something, and the choir sang.

The funeral was over now, and we went out to the cemetery to watch my mom lowered into her grave. My tears had run dry by then. I was mostly silent and numb throughout the whole process. I stared at my mom's obituary. It had a pretty picture of her when she was younger. It was taken before she had me, I think, and it was amazing to me that they even had that picture. I wonder where they found it. The limo ride home was long. It felt like it took longer to get home than it did to get to the funeral. Everybody got out at the Rogers' house.

"Calvin, we're having dinner. Would you like to stay and eat with us?" Mrs. Rogers asked him.

"Oh! No, thank you. We'll just be on our way home," Calvin responded in a raspy tone.

I interjected and said, "No, I wanna stay and eat."

Calvin kind of tensed up, but whatever he wanted to let out, he kept in. He pursed his lips and said, "That's fine. I'll come get you tomorrow." Then he slowly walked out to his car and drove off.

Danny stood there with me as we both watched Calvin disappear out of my life, as simple as that. As we silently walked into the house together, Mrs. Rogers asked me, "Do you want to eat dinner, NaNida?"

"Yes, yes I do," I answered her.

"Well, go wash up and get yourself together. We'll all have dinner," she said with a smile on her face.

I put a smile on my face as well and headed upstairs. I had some clothes over there already from previous stays. I sorted through my clothes for something comfortable to wear. Once I found it I took a nice, hot shower and let the water rinse my tears away. Memories of

Theresa were going through my mind. I had no one now. No family at all. The closet thing I had to family was the Rogers and Calvin. It was sad to admit, but it was true.

When I got out the shower and got myself together, I went to the guest room where I slept. I stared at the bed for a minute, lost in my thoughts. I finally snapped out of it, got on my knees, and prayed.

"Dear God, I would like to thank you for all of the good you put in my life and getting me through all the bad. I pray that you forgive Calvin and you help me to forgive him too for everything he's done to me and all the evil he caused in my life. I ask that you bless the Rogers for helping me and always being there," I said with a smile on my face as Danny came to mind. "I also ask that you watch over Danny. He's the only person I have left to love now. And you let my mother know that I will always love and remember her." I started to let the tears roll down my face as I continued. "Let her know that she can come visit me anytime she wants and if nobody else loved her, I did. She can be beautiful again and not have to worry about Calvin no more."

I paused for a couple of seconds.

"I also ask that you connect me with my father somehow. I need to find him. I need to know him, God, please. I need to know who he is. In Jesus' name I pray. Amen."

As I turned around with tears falling down my face I saw that Mrs. Rogers was standing in the doorway. She had tears in her eyes also. She had been watching me the entire time I was praying. The door was still half-way closed, so I guess that's why I didn't hear or see her at first. She opened the door all the way so I could see the man standing next to her.

"I have someone I want you to meet," she said.

I stared at him in wonderment. A buzz was going through my little body, and I couldn't figure out why. The man in the doorway was the same man who was staring at me during the funeral. He started to tear up looking at me. He finally let a smile grace his face and said, "I'm your uncle. I've been searching for you, and your father has too."

I was surprised and happy at the same time. I thought he was going to say that he was my father because why else would he be at the funeral? Why was he standing in that doorway with Mrs. Rogers and not my father?

"Where is he?" I asked.

"He's here. He's waiting for you," my uncle replied.

A confused look came across on my face.

"Come on," Mrs. Rogers said as she grabbed my hand.

She led me down the stairs to the living room. When we got there I saw a man with the exact same face as mine. He was just older and manly looking, plus he was in a wheelchair, which explained a lot.

"Oh my God, we found you. We found you," he whispered into the air.

I could see the tears beginning to form in his eyes. Mine were tearing up too. I rushed to his arms even though I didn't really know him yet. While he held me in a bear hug, he whispered to me that he was my father and never wanted to lose me again. He wasn't Italian. He was mixed with black and white, and he sure wasn't in prison like my mom had told me he was. I knew the words he spoke to me were true. I almost couldn't believe it. I finally had a father. I finally had someone I knew as my real father, and I also know that everything my mom had told me was a lie. We had missed out on eleven years together. We had eleven years' worth of catching up to do.

God had answered my prayers. Calvin was out of my life, my mom was finally off drugs, she didn't have to deal with Calvin and his beatings, and *I* finally had a father!

Out Soon...

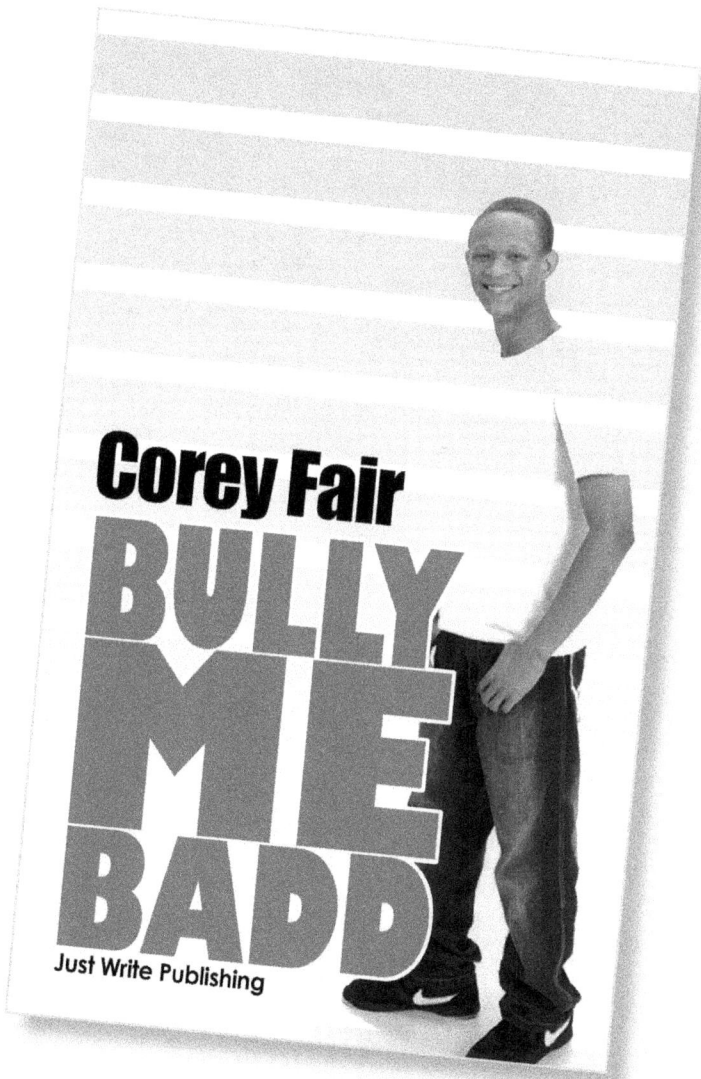

Corey Fair

BULLY ME BADD

Just Write Publishing

BULLY ME BADD

Corey Fair

Just Write Publishing

BULLY ME BADD

PROLOGUE

A lot of people often wonder how I became the way I am. And what way would that be, you may ask yourself. Well, I'm violent and physically and mentally abusive to both strangers *and* people who love me. I'm also a criminal. According to the law.

I wasn't born like this though. I was made into the person I am today. Bullied into it, actually. I was constantly harassed by schoolmates, older siblings, and people who didn't even know me. But now I'm the bully. It's not something that I'm proud of, but it's also nothing I'm embarrassed about either. It's just how things turned out.

I grew up with my older brother and cousins, and my grandmother raised us. My mom died in a car crash while she was pregnant. I guess it messed my father up so much that he got turned out on dope. So there was no one else to raise me except my brother and cousins. And only my grandmother was really there for me. So... let me tell you how I became "this way."

BULLY ME BADD

CHAPTER

01

I GUESS I'LL START AT THE BEGINNING. Well, at least the beginning that I remember. I wish I could tell you sweet, mushy stories about how we were a nice, happy family before my mom died and my father got addicted to heroin. But I can't. I was only three, and truth be told, when you're three years old and a person is not consistently in your life, you forget them and the memories you had of them. So, let me get straight to the story of my first bully encounter.

When I was four years old, I went to this big day care. I remember it being called Small Soldiers. We watched a movie every week. And one particular week we watched a movie called *Dumbo*. It's about a young elephant who is born with extremely large ears, and he gets picked on by every other animal around him. Even the other elephants. Dumbo did have one friend though: a mouse. To everyone's surprise, it turns out that Dumbo is special. Dumbo was somebody. And that mouse helped him realize it. Little did I know I was watching the blueprint of my life.

There were two brothers, twins actually, who picked on me every day they could after we watched that movie in daycare. They would call me Dumbo, big ears, and stuff like that. They would point and laugh at me. They even got a couple of other kids to join in the fun of picking on me because of my ears.

I never retaliated or even showed any emotion in front of them, but once I got home, I would cry in private to my Granny about my ears. She would soothe me and make me feel good about myself. She would make me laugh about the whole situation, and I could shrug it off like it was nothing.

Until I saw the twins again. Then it would start all over again.

If I was anything like I am now, I would've crushed the twins' world and made them dread the sight of me. They were dusty. They had nappy hair. They always had crusty noses and they were black. And by black I don't mean "African American;" I mean dark as hell. If I was like I am now, I could have made them suffer.

But let's not get ahead of ourselves. You need to know what I was like before. Then I'll show you the monster I am now.

My name is Da'mond Pires. I was born in Memphis, Tennessee in the fabulous year of 1993. My family stayed in a suburban neighborhood in a city right outside of Memphis. I have an older brother named Charles who is four years older than me.

We're what you call "pretty boys," or, at least that's how I would like to see it. My brother and I both had brown hair and blue eyes. He was high yellow, and me? I was pale skin in the winter and slightly tan in the summer. I am diagnosed with a congenital disorder called albinism. My doctor said I was only partial albino because I actually took a slight tan in the summer. (Boy, did I like it when the good ole sun shined bright on my pale skin and darkened it up a bit). A lot of people mistake us for being mixed (black and white), but we are Cape Verdeans. Our family is from an island called Cape Verde approximately 350 miles off the coast of Western Africa in the Atlantic Ocean. We're Africans! My ancestors were shipped to the islands to work on Portuguese plantations.

Interesting Note: In Tanzania, the country that my ancestors are originally from (and approximately 4000 miles from Cape Verde), our own African people would hunt down albino children and cut off their body parts to sell them on the black market to witch doctors for thousands of dollars. It was believed that albinos carried some type of magical powers in their hair, skin, and blood. They believed (or still do) that the parts of an albino brought them riches, good luck, and other blessings.

My father came over to America to go to college. He graduated and met my mother Amber, a Cape Verdean woman. Later, he became the vice chairman of a company called Black Rock Investment Group, and they had my brother Charles. A few years later, they had me. Then not too long after I popped out, my mom was pregnant again. But my would-be sister (my granny would like to think the baby would have been a girl) would never have a chance to breathe life because my mom died in a deadly car crash in the summer of 1995.

Things then took a turn for the worst. My father started doing dope. And somewhere along the way, my brother and I got sent to Indianapolis, Indiana to live with our grandmother. We called her Nana.

She's our mom's mom. She was a teacher. So, naturally, she thought education was important. She made sure we were educated. She was also keen on appearance, so we stayed dapper. She was a devout Christian, so we stayed in church.

Nana put me in one of the best day cares in the area. She also bought me all kinds of learning tools to teach me to read, write, and everything else before I ever entered a kindergarten classroom. And that day care did more than give me a place to learn the alphabet. That place taught me so much more. It was where I was first introduced to this act called bullying. This is where my horrible adventure began.